THE GREEN MAN

Carving of the Green Man at Fountains Abbey, Yorkshire

THE GREEN MAN

Kathleen Basford

D. S. BREWER

First published 1978
Reprinted 1996
D. S. Brewer, Cambridge

ISBN 0 85991 024 5

D. S. Brewer is an imprint of Boydell & Brewer Ltd
PO Box 9, Woodbridge, Suffolk IP12 3DF, UK
and of Boydell & Brewer Inc.
PO Box 41026, Rochester, NY 14604-4126, USA

British Library Cataloguing in Publication Data
Basford, Kathleen
    The green man
        1. Carving (Decorative arts) 2. Foliate head (sculpture)
        3. Christian art and symbolism - Medieval, 500-1500
        4. Sculpture, Medieval - Themes, motives
    I. Title
    729.5
    ISBN 0 859910254

Printed in Great Britain by
Whitstable Litho Printers Ltd., Whitstable, Kent.

CONTENTS

TOKUMI AYZEN,

Who loves the Green Man

PERSONAL PREFACE

The medieval churches and cathedrals of Western Europe are full of fantastic images. This is the story of one of them – the foliate head, a face or mask with leaves sprouting from it which we, in Britain, nowadays call the Green Man.[1, 2, 3, 4]

The Green Man is probably the most common decorative motif of medieval sculpture that has been left to us. It can be found on roof bosses, capitals, corbels, fonts, tombs, tympana, screens, bench ends, poppy heads, misericords and arm rests. It was a remarkably adaptable motif: it could be manipulated to fit any space or position where ornament was required. It could be introduced to enrich, enliven and bring variety into a scheme of leaf decoration and there provide, like a fantastic flower, a focal point of interest, or it could be made to blend into its leafy surroundings so inconspicuously that only the most perceptive eye could distinguish it from pure foliage. It would be used to form a centre for a discrete leaf cluster or a source from which long sprays of foliage might flow out as water from the head of a fountain. The idea of a face in the leaves could excite an imaginative response, and the individual craftsman could improvise on the theme and create his own fanciful variation of the motif.

Many of these carvings are sinister. Some of them are powerful fantasies of the eerie and macabre. There are very few benevolent or serenely smiling faces: more typically they frown. The eyes glare balefully or stare, unfocused, into space, full of dark foreboding. Sometimes the eyes are squinting, the expressions suggesting various levels of inebriation; bellicose, morose, even comatose, but seldom jocose. Sometimes, the faces are partially or almost wholly hidden behind the leaves they bear, secret faces, peering through gaps in the foliage.

It was the discovery of such faces under the leaves, carved on roof bosses in the Lady Chapel of Ely Cathedral that first suggested a resemblance to the Green Man, or Jack in the Green, peeping through the leaves with which he was covered when he played his part in the ceremonies on May Day.[5]

Although the Jack in the Green explanation cannot be stretched to fit and cover every example of the motif as it was used in the Middle Ages (it may not even precisely fit any of them), the image does, in fact, display at least one Green Man characteristic, namely, his power of revival and regeneration.

Images may pick up many different ideas during the course of time. They can evolve and diversify as they are exposed to different cultural climates and as they catch the imagination of the particular individuals who use them. Visual images, no less than written documents, can give valuable insights into the thoughts, ideas and even dreams of people who made them.[6]

The foliate head attracted many different ideas into its sphere during its long history and each example can be studied as a historical document, reflecting some of the thoughts that shaped it at a particular place and at a particular time, and also as a personal document, left to us by an individual craftsman who, though he may have sometimes been an illiterate man, unable to put his thoughts and feelings into writing, could express the strangest and most subtle ideas in his carving.

My personal quest for the Green Man began with a chance and quite unexpected encounter with the foliate head at Fountains Abbey in Yorkshire. One day, while wandering round the ruins,

I happened to glance up at one of the tall windows of the Chapel of the Nine Altars and notice, near the apex of the arch, the carving of a human head with a weird growth of vegetation coming out of the mouth. It caught my attention because there is so little else in the way of imagery or decorative sculpture at Fountains. Even during the later period of its history this Abbey maintained its austere Cistercian character and so this solitary Green Man, the only ornament of any kind on the outside wall of the Chapel, took me by surprise.

The stone on which the figure is carved was inserted late in the fifteenth century to repair the damage due to settlement.[7] Although the introduction of a foliate head may have been an innovation and something of an anomaly at Fountains it was a long-established motif in church architecture and its use here at this time would probably not have seemed remarkable, much less revolutionary. The choice of this rather than any other common motif may well have been determined by the fact that it was the one which could most easily be shaped to fit the situation and cover an awkward join, but the mason made something very personal and moving of his ornamental patchwork.

The sad face of this withered old man seemed to me the most human touch left in the ruins and yet, at the same time, the most ghostly. It reminded me of the Echo image in Webster's *Duchess of Malfi*. The echo, "the best echo that you ever heard", was the only remaining "life" in the ruins of the old abbey which Antonio, the hero, visited just before his death, with his friend Delio, and to every sentence spoken it gave a deadly accent.

Antonio	. . . all things have their end:
	Churches and Cities (which have diseases like to men)
	Must have like death that we have.
Echo	*Like death that we have.*
Delio	Now the Echo hath caught you.
Antonio	It groan'd (me thought) and gave
	A very deadly accent?
Echo	*Deadly accent.*
Delio	I told you 'twas a pretty one. You may make it
	A huntsman, or a falconer, or a musician
	Or a thing of sorrow.
Echo	*A thing of sorrow.*
Antonio	Aye sure, that suits it best.

The Green Man, caught up in the branches like the severed head of a felon, makes a very deadly accent on the walls of Fountains. It certainly could not be interpreted as a Jack in the Green. Not only would a Jack in the Green make nonsense in this strictly monastic church but the derelict head, invaded and taken over by vegetation, is an image of death and ruin rather than that of life and resurrection. It is, indeed, "a thing of sorrow". That suits it best.

I began to wonder if the craftsman could make what he liked of the motif, "a huntsman, a falconer, or a musician" or whatever it was that the idea of a face in the leaves suggested to him. Why should it have suggested an image of human ruin?

But I had picked up the Green Man story at a point when the motif was near the end of its life in the Church and in order to understand this one isolated fragment I had to go back and try to follow the story from the beginning.

Drawing of carving on the base of the lid of St Abre's tomb, Poitiers; 4th or 5th century.

THE HISTORY AND DEVELOPMENT OF THE GREEN MAN

(i) Prototypes of the Green Man in antique and early medieval ornament

The foliate head, or leaf mask, from which the Green Man ultimately derives, appeared in Roman art during the second half of the first century A.D.,[8, 9] but it is generally considered rather as a second century motif since this was the period of its formal development. It was sometimes used as a repeated motif in the "peopled scroll" ornament, and sometimes as an isolated motif. Male masks with acanthus scrolls sprouting from their faces were reproduced on friezes on both triumphal arches of Septimius Severus in Rome and on Aurelian's Temple of the Sun, also in Rome,[10] but the motif was widespread throughout the eastern and western parts of the Empire, and examples are found as far apart as Baalbek[11, 12] and Bordeaux.[13] It was used on temples serving many different deities and also on sarcophagi, in much the same way as the medusa mask.

The motif has, in fact, been described as a male medusa,[14] and one example, carved in high relief on the façade of a temple at Hatra in Mesopotamia[15] (the modern Al Hadr, Iraq) has snakes writhing in his hair. The Hatra mask bears a remarkable resemblance to the glowering male medusa on the pediment of the temple at Sulis Minerva at Bath,[16] though this is not a leaf mask. The Bath medusa has also been compared with the scowling Okeanos mask on the central medallion of the great silver dish from Mildenhall (now in the British Museum).[17] Like the Hatra mask, the Mildenhall Okeanos has a beard of seaweed or acanthus, but has dolphins instead of snakes swimming through his wild, wavy locks. The penetrating glare, common to all three masks, is a persistent though not invariable characteristic of the antique leaf masks and must be recognised as a "family trait", later inherited by the Green Men.

Other, quite different prototypes of the Green Man are found on several fragments from the richly sculptured funerary monuments discovered at Neumagen, on the Mosel, not far from Trier.[18]

The monuments, which date from the second and third centuries, were made to commemorate distinguished and wealthy Treveran citizens, many of whom were wine merchants, and some of the splendid sarcophagi are actually in the form of wine ships, manned by a crew of sailors – some of them very merry.

The leaf masks, which appear on fragments from four of these memorials have been cited as being among the most important for the development of motif in countries north of the Alps.[19] One of them almost certainly represents Okeanos who, in this context, would symbolise a safe and prosperous voyage to the Islands of the Blessed. The meaning of the others is not so clear. The leaf mask which is the central feature of a large sculptured panel from the *Iphigenienpfeiler* has, on one side of it, a cymbal with a shepherd's crook stuck through it,[20] and these objects may have Bacchic significance since the maenads clashed cymbals and satyrs carried crooked sticks.[21] It is tempting to wonder if the leaf mask also refers to some aspect of the Bacchic cult, and perhaps recalls the ancient rustic festivals held in honour of Dionysos revellers stained their faces with new wine and masked them with huge beards made out of leaves.[22] On the other hand, Okeanos is often used side by side with Bacchic themes, so this leaf mask might well represent Okeanos.

The Neumagen leaf masks are very variable in form and range from the type in which the leafy element is subordinate to the human element – reduced to a mere frill of acanthus beard and whisker on the fleshy chin and cheeks, and a curly acanthus eyebrow, to the type where the human face is completely veiled by acanthus (as on the *Iphigenienpfeiler*) with the leaves not only substituting for the facial hair but also growing from the tear glands in the corners of the eyes and from the inside of the mouth, and, finally, to the type which is all leaves – the human element suggested by the folding and overlapping of the deeply lobed acanthus.

Two faces representative of this extreme type are discovered in a frieze from the *Schulreliefpfeiler*. The frieze is filled with sensitively carved acanthus and the faces are formed, it would seem, as though by a chance arrangement of the leaves. Yet they are so skillfully portrayed that although nothing remains of human flesh they are full of human feeling. How can a cluster of leaves seem so grief-stricken? Perhaps because, in this complete metamorphosis, it is suggested that the sad faces are no more than a memory.

The fragments of the Neumagen monuments are now in the Rheinisches Landesmuseum in Trier, and here also are two casts taken from the splendid second century leaf masks which were introduced into Trier Cathedral in the sixth century.

*The casts are the only visible evidence we have today of these leaf masks since the originals are walled up in the Cathedral behind masonry erected during the course of restoration in the eleventh century. They were discovered about a hundred years ago when excavations were carried out at the time of a further restoration.[23] The temporary removal of part of the eleventh century masonry gave access to one of the four pillars set up in the Square Chancel by Bishop Nicetius in the sixth century. The lavishly carved composite capital had, for its principal ornament, a huge leaf mask on each face, between the volutes. The cast, taken at the time of this brief exposure, shows a leaf-crowned head, with more leaves spreading over the brow and growing on the cheeks, from under the eyes and from the sides of the nose. The upper lip has been broken and because of this damage the expression of the face is somewhat distorted, but the great eyes, rolling up under the leafy brows, show that it was a deeply serious expression.

At the time of the nineteenth century excavations it was believed that the capitals were contemporary with the sixth century pillars and had been carved by Italian craftsmen working from Byzantine models. This dating was generally accepted until 1962[24] and although the capitals had

---

* Since I worked at Trier a small window has been inserted into the wall, so that visitors can now glimpse the Green Man. I am grateful to William Anderson for this information.

been tentatively attributed to the second century by one earlier authority[25] this date was not finally confirmed until the excavations of 1961–63[26] when the original material was re-examined and subjected to a more critical scrutiny. The capitals were studied with particular reference to archaeological findings made on the site of Hadrianic temple, known as "Am Herrenbrünnchen".[27] Their style and material corresponded to the style and material of other sculptured fragments discovered on that site, and their measurements showed that they would have exactly fitted the pillars of the portico of the temple. It was therefore concluded that they had originally belonged to it and that Bishop Nicetius had recovered them from the ruins and used them, at second hand, for his new pillars in the Cathedral. Once installed in their new position, the capitals were painted in bright colours, the leaf masks and volutes golden yellow and the acanthus ornament below them red. Traces of pigment could still be seen on the capital when the second cast was made at the time of the 1861–63 excavations.

It must be assumed that Bishop Nicetius had admired the excellent workmanship and sumptuous splendour of these figured capitals and had chosen them for these qualities and not for their particular subject matter. The foliate head came into the Cathedral, as it were, by accident. But it was no doubt an event of great importance for the motif and probably marked a turning point in its history.

The beautiful leaf mask capitals were displayed for five hundred years in Trier Cathedral. The casts can give us only a grey and rather ghostly reflection of their magnificence. The pillars on which they were mounted stood, one at each corner of the Square Chancel, an area of special sanctity which was built in the fourth century and planned round a curious architectural feature[28] which is thought to have been repository for some precious relic, perhaps a fragment of the True Cross or perhaps the Seamless Robe which is now preserved in the Cathedral Treasury.

In Trier, the leaf mask began its new life in the service of the church in particularly auspicious and favourable circumstances. Sanctioned by long use in this venerable church in one of the earliest and most important strongholds of Christianity in the West it could pass easily into medieval ornament.

While we may suppose that it was probably this chance induction into the Cathedral in Trier that gave the foliate head a secure place in the church, we cannot be sure that, but for this happy accident, it would not have survived. Even before Bishop Nicetius had adopted it, the motif had found a small niche in Christian ornament.

A foliate head is carved in shallow relief on the base of the marble lid of the tomb of Sainte-Abre in the Church of Saint-Hilaire-le-Grand in Poitiers.[29, 30] This Christian tomb, which dates from the fourth or fifth century, is decorated with motifs borrowed from pagan tombs. They include dolphins, a rayed bust, and a vase containing foliage as well as the foliate head. It is a curious carving, quite unlike the Hellenistic leaf masks. The head is surrounded by contiguous and over-lapping leaves which may represent the hair and beard, while large sprays of stylised foliage and flowers spring from the nostrils and extend on either side of the head, like fantastic moustaches. This modest work is of great interest, not only because it is such an early example in Christian ornament, but because of its originality. It does not so much look backward to the Hellenistic leaf masks from which it undoubtedly derives as forward, perhaps providing a prototype for the early medieval figures with leaves, or leafy tendrils or branches coming out of the nostrils.

There are no foliate heads, nor other fantastic creatures in the eastern church. This is possibly explained by the fact that from the eighth century there was strong opposition to the use of imagery. The absence of the motif certainly cannot be explained by any lack of inspiring models. There is much evidence to show that the leaf mask was a popular architectural ornament in Constantinople and in other places round the Bosphoros and the Sea of Marmora in the fifth and sixth centuries. Beautiful examples in the Hellenistic tradition were still being produced in this region at the very time that the motif was beginning its new lease of life in the western church. Several figured capitals, all of them dating from the sixth century, with leaf masks as their only, or dominant motif can be seen today in the Archaeological Museum in Istanbul. The finest example in this collection was discovered at Mudanya on the southern shores of the Sea of Marmora in 1885. The leaf masks are situated at the angles on one side of the capital and between them is a horn of plenty which has an acanthus leaf at the base and grapes brimming over the lip and, suspended above, a leaf from the plane tree with a ripe pod on the left of it and an ear of wheat on the right. The masks have been described as figures of Okeanos under a type which is, at once, satyr and sea god.[31] The hair, eyebrows, whiskers, moustache and beard are all formed from acanthus. The faces have both strength and delicacy and an expression of sombre gravity. The forehead is slightly furrowed and the eyes, with their deeply incised pupils, stare out into space and seem preoccupied with inner vision.

A second capital, of unknown provenance, has leaf masks of the satyr type, one on each of its four faces. Two large acanthus leaves, growing from either side of a narrow vertical fold of flesh just above the nose, rise up to form the moustache, while a fifth leaf, growing from under the full lip, hangs down over the chin to form the beard. The face is clearly indicated as a mask, cut off in a straight line across the forehead, and yet this mask-like appearance is contradicted by the intensity of the expression: the curiously elongated eyes, with their barely focused pupils, have a look of rapt introspection.

Two leaf masks, one on each of a pair of capitals found in Istanbul on the site now occupied by the New Palace of Justice, are represented with the pupils of the eyes converging in a quite definite squint.

The horn of plenty appears again side by side with leaf masks on a capital discovered in the old City Wall in 1972. This second example may indicate that the juxtaposition of the two motifs was more than mere coincidence.

Very few of the foliated figures in the manuscripts and carvings of the tenth, eleventh and twelfth centuries bear any close resemblance to the leaf masks of antiquity; throughout this period the leaf mask is mainly represented as a demon. The change of character is clearly illustrated in two manuscripts produced either at Reichenau or Trier about the year 980.[32] The first of these[33] was presented to Egbert, Archbishop of Trier in 983. The dedicatory miniature is framed by a border of human masks linked together by an acanthus scroll. The idea is obviously derived from the leaf masks in the Hellenistic "peopled scroll" motif, but the faces are rather goblin-like and the foliage sprouts from the mouth and not from the cheeks. In the border of the corresponding dedication page of the second manuscript,[34] presented to Egbert two years later, the human masks are replaced by horrific hollow demon masks with snakes and birds coming our of their ears. The scroll is a complex of foliage, birds and beasts, one form growing out of another – even the leaves have become demonic.

The thoughts that lie behind this change can probably be traced to Rabanus Maurus, an erudite and influential theologian of the eighth century. According to him, the leaves represented the sins of the flesh or lustful and wicked men doomed to eternal damnation.[35]

The evil aspect of the leaf mask is nowhere more dramatically expressed than in the carving on the façade of San Pietro, Toscanella (Tuscania), Viterbo. It is, basically, a type of "peopled-scroll" ornament, framing an open, colonnaded window. The leafy scrolls issue from two monstrous masks centrally placed in the upper and lower borders of the frame. Both masks are in the form of a tricephalos, a head with three faces, one presented in frontal view, the other two in profile. Each face has its own mouth and nose, but shares with the others a single pair of eyes.

In medieval imagery the tricephalos could symbolise either the Holy Trinity or Absolute Evil.[36, 37] The two directly opposite iconological applications do not, of course, derive from one another, but each derives independently from a Gallo-Roman prototype (extremely common in the region of Reims). There can be no doubt which of these meanings is intended at Toscanella.

The two monsters are similar but not identical. In both cases the centre face sticks his tongue out while the faces in profile stick out, not a fleshy tongue, but a long "tongue" of foliated scroll. Each demon has, however, his own diabolical attributes: the upper one is horned and the lower one, which is attached to a torso, clasps a serpent to his bosom and the snake, like his master, sticks out his venomous tongue.

The imagery probably refers to the story of Christ's Descent into Hell as it was told in the apocryphal gospel of Nicodemus. This story, quoted in a Good Friday sermon preached by Eusebius of Alexandria in the sixth century, tells how the devil, thrown into confusion by the Crucifixion, fled in panic to hell to shut the gates to prevent Christ's entry into the infernal regions, but he, with his angels, followed in pursuit and demanded admittance: "*Lift up your heads, O ye gates; and be ye lift up ye everlasting doors; and the King of glory shall come in*" Ps. 24.7. Christ confronted Satan at the threshold and addressed him as τριχέφαλε Βεελζεβούλ (translated as *triceps Beelzebub* in a fifteenth century manuscript) – Three headed Beelzebub.[38, 39] In the same apocryphal gospel Satan is called *radix omnium malorum*, Root of All Evil.[40] The coiling tendrils that push out through the mouths of the threefaced demons may well be explained as suckers springing up from the evil root below.

The demons of early medieval art are frequently portrayed with the tongue, the "unruly member", sticking out. A demon head on a capital at Avignon not only sticks his tongue out but also displays savage teeth. The demon mouth may sometimes signify the Jaws of Hell, and on a capital in the cathedral at Autun the body of a man is seen disappearing in the jaws of a leaf mask.

Twelfth century leaf masks are seldom represented with the foliage actually growing on the face. A mask of this type, carved on a corbel at Königslutter and dating from 1135, is one of the rare exceptions. Far more common are the types with foliage – foliated scrolls, slender tendrils or thicker branches – coming out of the mouth and nose. It seems possible that these forms developed as extreme modifications of the foliate moustache (the leaf mask on the tomb of Sainte-Abre in Poitiers may anticipate this development) but they must be recognised as distinct types in medieval art. Perhaps the branches growing out of these masks may always be referred back to the dark root of evil but it has been pointed out that the faces with leaves coming out of the nose can have a more specific meaning,[41] and can be interpreted in accordance with the text: *See, how they hold the branch to the nose.* Ezekiel 8.17, and allude to the idolaters to whom God would show no mercy. It is not always possible to distinguish between the demons and the damned (who also belong to the Devil). Sometimes snakes or dragons come out of the mouth instead of leaves but, as we have seen, in early medieval art branches may freely change into diabolical beasts or birds and it is not improbable that they all sprout from a common root stock.

The mask itself is capable of changing into animal form. The most common variant of the human mask is the cat mask. The foliate cat mask is frequently seen in the decorated initials of manuscripts, very often the Beatus initial of the Psalter where it forms the bar between the bows of the letter B, but it seems to be readily interchangeable with the human form which is also used in this way as, for example, in the Folkunge Psalter,[42] in the Royal Library in Copenhagen.

The cat mask is reproduced on a capital, dating from 1120, in St. Kyneburga's, Castor, near Peterborough. In this carving it is, apparently, an anthropomorphic feline since it grasps the branches coming out of the mouth with human hands.

The basic type of Romanesque leaf mask is also represented at Castor in its two most common forms, one with the foliage coming out of the mouth, the other with foliage coming from the nose. In spite of all its bizarre shape shifting the motif can almost always be recognised with reference to one of these forms.

St. Bernard of Clairvaux,[43] who deplored the extravagant use of grotesque imagery in the Cluniac monasteries, did not specifically mention the figures with leaves sprouting from their faces in his inventory of "admirable deformed beauties and beautiful deformities", but many of them would qualify for inclusion among the "unclean apes".

The usual place for leaf masks (and other "beautiful deformities") in Romanesque churches is on capitals, but they are also found on corbels, fonts and tympana. If, however, sacred subjects are also represented on the tympanum the leaf mask is placed in a separate, usually clearly defined zone, such as the border. A possible exception of this general rule appears at Elkstone, Gloucestershire.[44] The figures represented on the tympanum include Christ enthroned, his right hand raised in a gesture of blessing, his left hand holding the Book of Judgement; the symbols of the four evangelists; the *Agnus Dei*, signifying the Passion of Christ, and an angel in the corner on the right hand side of Christ while in the corner on the left hand side of Christ is "a grotesque from the mouth of which comes a scroll of leaf ornament". This grotesque may certainly be recognised as a leaf mask. The foliated scrolls coming from his mouth extend to frame the other figures so this apparent "maverick" may, after all, represent the border. It does, however, occupy the position which, in scenes of the Last Judgement, is often filled by sinners, rejected by Christ and on their way to Hell.

One of the best known leaf masks in English Romanesque sculpture is the demon on a capital of the south doorway of Kilpeck church, in Herefordshire. The branches – probably stylised vine – coming out of his mouth bear both leaves and fruit.

The same plant motif appears on the tympanum. It may, in this case, be a purely decorative motif, not intended to represent the Tree of Life,[45] but, were such an interpretation permissible, Tree of Life symbolism could have a particular significance in relation to the demon. The Tree of Life was also the tree from which Eve plucked the forbidden fruit (sometimes she takes the fruit directly from the jaws of the serpent).[46] It could be *Arbor mala* as well as *Arbor bona*.[47]

Although it is not possible to explain every individual example of the fantastic leaf mask – some of the fantasy is, no doubt, purely decorative, and explanations of particular "grotesques" must always be offered with extreme caution yet, collectively, their meaning in quite clear: they are demons and spectres of the demon wood. A tradition of meaning was established for the motif in the early Middle Ages and our problem, and adventure, is to discover what new ideas expanded the range of meaning as the fantasy was spun out in the thirteenth, fourteenth and fifteenth centuries to produce the Green Man.

(ii) *The era of the Green Man*

Early in the thirteenth century the style of leaf ornament changed, and the foliate head, which was used as a variant form of leaf ornament, changed correspondingly. Quite distinct changes of style occurred in France, Germany and England, but gradually the French style influenced the development of the motif in the other two countries, first in Germany and later, towards the end of the century, in England.

Before considering these changes, mention must be made of a foliate head which, though it clearly belongs to the Green Man story, represents an exceptional, possibly unique episode in it.

It is carved on the basin of a fountain made in or about the year 1200 for the Cloisters of the Abbey of Saint-Denis and is one of a series of heads, each one representing a different Roman deity. Every head has the name of the god inscribed above it, and the name given to the leaf mask is Silvan.[48]

The Silvanus of Saint Denis is a iconographical puzzle since Silvanus was never represented in the form of a leaf mask in antiquity and there is no evidence to suggest that the motif was widely known as Silvanus in the Middle Ages. It has oak leaves growing from the brow and is rather similar to the Bacchus figure illustrated in the Encyclopaedia of Rabanus Maurus.[49] It would seem, therefore, that the artist had simply imagined the old woodland god in this way, and used the motif to express his own idea.

The foliate heads of thirteenth century France are of two main types, distinguished by the differences in their formal structure, and known respectively as the *Tête de Feuilles* and the *Masque Feuillu*. Four examples of the *Tête de Feuilles* are illustrated in the book of architectural notes and drawings made by the master mason Villard de Honnecourt about the year 1235.[50] He shows two kinds of "metamorphosis": human faces changing into leaves (the head on a human neck and shoulders), and leaves changing into human faces (in one case, a cluster of leaves and in the other, a single leaf on a stalk). He calls them all by the purely descriptive name *Tête de* Feuilles.

Drawings of *Têtes de Feuilles* after Villard de Honnecourt, 1235.

In the *Tête de Feuilles*, as in the leaf masks of antiquity, the human and leafy elements are fused into one "organic" whole, and so differs from the other type of foliate head common in the thirteenth century in which the two elements remain distinct entities no matter how intimately they may be interwoven. Since Villard de Honnecourt did not illustrate this type we do not know whether or not the would have called it a *Tête de Feuilles* too, but it is now generally called a *Masque Feuillu* (occasionally *Masque Herbu)* in recognition of the somewhat different structure. The *Tête de Feuilles* derives directly from the antique leaf masks whereas the Masque Feuillu derives partly from the early medieval leaf demons with foliated tendrils and branches coming from the mouth or nose. The two types cannot, however, be regarded as two distinct motifs because intermediate forms can be found partly of one type, partly of the other; they tend to converge and overlap rather that to diverge and become two separate "species".

Both types are represented, side by side, in a group of three foliate heads above the portal of the south transept of Chartres cathedral. The single *Tête de Feuilles* (an acanthus mask) has, on each side of it, a *Masque Feuillu* – one with vines coming out of the mouth, and other with oak. The oak and vine leaves are carved realistically; not only are the leaves accurately portrayed but the natural habit of growth, the leaf mosaic – the pattern formed by the leaves as each turns on its stem to find a place in the light – has also been observed. Such careful and sensitive observation of nature is a remarkable innovation of thirteenth century sculpture.

Drawing of *Têtes de Feuilles* after Villard de Honnecourt, 1235.

The *Tête de Feuilles* was often chosen, as an alternative to pure foliage, to fill the space between or at the sides of arches. The two leaf masks used as "space fillers" on the inner west wall of Reims cathedral are very similar to the *Tête de Feuilles* in the form of a single leaf drawn by Villard de Honnecourt. A most elegant example of the *Tête de Feuilles* used as the filling in a spandrel is seen in the choir screen of Poitiers cathedral, and another on the shrine of Saint Étienne, in the Abbey church at Aubazine (Corrèze). But the *Tête de Feuilles* was used in many other ways: it could be developed as a three-dimensional design, as on a corbel in Auxerre cathedral. This lovely carving shows a head of leaves disturbed by the wind (and perhaps also by some uneasy, restless spirit).

The *Masque Feuillu* was used as the source or centre of a spreading, or extended scheme of leaf decoration: the luxurious vines wreathed round capitals in the chancel of Notre Dame, Sémur-en-Auxios and the leafy tendrils spiralling on the roof bosses in the Chapter House of Noyon cathedral all rise out the mouths of human heads. (The heads on the roof bosses at Noyon are among the first to look like teasing Jack in the Greens). The demon nature of the motif was not, however, forgotten. A horned leaf demon appears in the corner of the lintel of the portal of Saint-Urbain in Troyes, and is placed immediately beneath a dramatic representation of the Jaws of Hell. But the demonic character is never exaggerated. The foliate heads of the thirteenth century do not stick their tongues out nor expose fierce animal teeth as though about to eat us. The sinister side of their nature is usually expressed with subtlety. It is developed on the basis of the iconography of the antique leaf masks – the brooding frown, the glowering expression, and the look of dark foreboding.

Evidence for the use of the motif in secular ornament in the thirteenth century is scanty. It was engraved on a gold and enamel harness ornament, probably made in Limoges and now in the Cluny Museum in Paris. The *Tête de Feuilles* on this superb "horse-brass" has leafy eyebrows, moustache and whiskers, and almost squinting eyes.

Among the earliest of the thirteenth century leaf masks in Germany are the six heads interlaced with acanthus leaves in the border framing the late Romanesque tympanum over the market portal of Mainz cathedral, which dates from 1200 to 1215. The motif is used here in just the same way as in the previous century, but is not represented as a "grotesque". These leaf masks have been recognised as deriving directly from a Roman-provincial monument.[51] Likewise the mask (or masks?) on a capital of the forecourt portal of Maria Laach Abbey (*circa* 1230). Carved on two adjacent blocks of stone, two leaf masks almost, but not quite in profile, confront each other to become as one, in full face view.

A quite different type of leaf mask appears on a corbel in the church of St Peter and St Alexander in Aschaffenburg. It was carved in 1220 by the master mason Fingerhaut. Leaves grow on the forehead and on the chin and other leaves, probably vine, come out of the mouth. This face has a little fold or wrinkle of flesh above the bridge of the nose. This feature, also shown in two of Villard de Honnecourt's drawings, is a character "inherited" from antique prototypes (it is seen, for example, in the Okeanos-satyr masks on the Mudanya capital).

Faces formed wholly of leaves appear in German sculpture during the third decade of the century. Splendid examples of this extreme form of the motif are found in the Marienkirche in Gelnhausen and in Bamberg cathedral.

The Bamberg leaf mask is carved on one side of the console under the statue of the mounted Knight, known as The Rider. It has been said of this carving: "The foliage comes to life as a huge acanthus leaf is transformed into the features of a man. . . . The noble expression of the face, the mastery of form and grandeur bring it into relationship with the Knight whose character it reflects",[52] yet it is not an exact reflection of the Holy Knight, but rather his dark counterpart. All the darkness and power and mystery of a vast forest seem concentrated in this majestic head of leaves. The Bamberg leaf mask is a Prince of Darkness.

The magnificent sculpture, dated 1237, is the work of the Bamberg Master. The leaf mask – the most beautiful foliate head of the thirteenth century, and perhaps of all time – is wholly German in character. The two oak leaf masks on the portal of Kloster Ebrach are, on the other hand, much closer to the French style and are, in fact very similar to the faces changing into leaves drawn by Villard de Honnecourt. Each is used as a substitute for pure foliage, one on the keystone of the arch and the other on one of the three bosses on the inner arches. It is, perhaps, because the motif was a variant form of leaf ornament that it was acceptable on the doorway of this Cistercian church as early as the thirteenth century. The discreet use of the leaf ornament was permitted at this time even in the most austere buildings.

The face on the boss is extremely emaciated and seems to have been sucked dry by the greedy leaves growing on it. Some of the leaves have oak galls on them – an interesting and possibly significant detail. It is difficult to believe that this ornament was entirely devoid of meaning. The expression suggests bitter disillusionment: so might a sinner, near to death, reflect on his wasted life.

> "So here's a thought your teeth should clench
> 'All greenness comes to withering' ".
>   13th century English verse.[53]

There is no hint of withering in the oak leaf that is placed, like a flower, among the prolific vines on the tympanum above the sacristy door in the Liebfrauenkirche in Friedburg. This late thirteenth century carving (dated *circa* 1290) further illustrates the ornamental value of the motif. The touch of fantasy among the otherwise naturalistic plant forms enhances the decorative quality of the whole design.

The foliate heads in English sculpture of the mid-thirteenth century are quite unlike any of the contemporary French or German types. The foliage is predominantly "stiff-leaf" (the examples at Much Marcle, Herefordshire, are dated 1260). Some have bizarre characteristics, for example, a mouth in the form of an infinity symbol (or a figure of eight). This weirdly exaggerated feature is seen in foliate heads in Ripon Cathedral and Dorchester Abbey. The head at Dorchester (Oxfordshire) has vines coming from each side of the huge mouth, and the twisted tendrils curve over the brow to frame the face, and although they are represented as growing upward from the stems they nevertheless simulate "hair", growing down from a central parting on the head: this detail can be visualised in two ways.

It is not until the late thirteenth century that naturalistic carving of native wild plants – hawthorn, hops, buttercup, maple, mugwort, bryony and ivy as well as oak appear in English churches. The most beautiful leaf carvings in England are found in the Chapter House of Southwell Minster, Nottinghamshire.[54] The foliate head is represented nine times, each time a little differently, in the Southwell Chapter House, but all the carvers' interest and skill is concentrated on the leaves and the heads are treated somewhat perfunctorily. All but one of them is in the form of the *Masque Feuillu*, preferred perhaps because it could serve so well as a source from which leafy sprays could pour out. More than one kind of plant could be placed in these convenient "vases": buttercup and hops together; bryony and wild apple; ivy and maple.[55] One small head simply looks through a bent-over spray of hawthorn. It was probably placed there to give the design a "centre". The heads are used to vary the decoration and perhaps have no specific meaning: if they are leaf demons they are not the aggressive kind, nor are the tiny dragons with linked hawthorn tails.

The single *Tête de Feuilles* at Southwell is a hawthorn mask. It is placed on the abacus above a capital decorated with flowering hawthorn – the may-blossom. The mask has one pair of leaves coming from the centre of the forehead and another pair on the chin. He has a small "fleur de lys" on his head, like a miniature crown. It is, of course, very tempting to interpret him as a May King, but we cannot be sure that this was his meaning.

The foliate head at Sutton Benger (Wiltshire) is also a hawthorn mask. A whole thicket – with birds pecking the berries – grows out of the mouth of the very sad face. This lovely carving, probably of the early fourteenth century, is everyone's idea of the Green Man. Comparison with the thirteenth century *Masque Feuillu* in Noyon Cathedral could indicate that the inspiration is French.

Such a carving might well suggest the idea of a Jack in the Green to a twentieth century observer, remembering the appearance of this character in May Day processions or recalling illustrations, such as the "Chimneysweeps' Jack o' the Green",[56] which show him covered down to his ankles by thick foliage mounted on a conical frame so that he looks like a walking, or dancing bower of leaves, with his beaming face peering out through a little peephole in the branches. But the resemblance could be quite fortuitous. Very little is known about the early history of the Jack in the Green," the name and the leafy structure appear together at the end of the eighteenth century in a context of May Day begging".[57]

The history and development of the Green Man in the Church can, on the other hand, be followed continuously from the fourth or fifth century. Though pagan in origin, the motif evolved within the Church and, during the early Middle Ages, became part of its symbolic language. The Green Man is mainly an ornamental development of the motif. He was developed in the thirteenth century through various modifications of the antique and early medieval forms and the use of foliage deriving from plants growing north of the Alps as well as acanthus. The greatest and most striking change in the motif, the change which particularly distinguishes him from his antique and early medieval prototypes, is the change in the leaves.

While it is possible that some of these leafy faces might allude to the May King or to the idea of the revival of nature in springtime, the Green Man more often evokes the horrors of the *silva daemonium*. A Green man who, at first glance, may seem the very personification of springtime, and "summer is i-comen in" may, on closer inspection, reveal himself as a nightmarish spectre. The imagery can be ambivalent. The Green Man can be at once both beautiful and sinister. The most beautiful of all, the thirteenth century acanthus mask in Bamberg cathedral, is also the most sinister.

The demonic character of the early medieval leaf masks certainly persists in many Green Man carvings. Some are portrayed as though "In gibe of goblin fantasy – Grimace – unclean diablerie",[58] but when the two components of the motif, face and foliage, are represented more naturalistically many new shades and slants of meaning become possible. The despair and anguish expressed in some of the faces is even more disquieting because it is so human. The evil is so much more frightening because it is human as well as diabolical. It is when the fantasy is expressed most naturalistically that it seems most eerie and touches us most powerfully.

The association between the human and plant elements is often suggested as an uneasy or actually hostile relationship rather than a balanced symbiosis. Sometimes the leaves appear parasitic, drawing their strength from the wretched head which bears them. A fifteenth century head from Melrose Abbey, now in the Abbey Museum is there labelled as a mask with "blood-suckers" at the eyes and mouth. I think the "blood-suckers" are vegetable: bloated leaf stalks. The carving may be compared with weird heads at Spreyton and at Sampford Courtenay in Devon, where the leaves seem like a morbid growth and blind the Green Man's eyes with a cataract-like membrane. Sometimes, even more horribly, leaves sprout from the pupils of the eyes. An example of this macabre feature is seen at Ottery St Mary, also in Devon.

Devon is one of the best of all the English counties for studying variations on the Green Man theme. There are at least seventeen Green Men in Exeter cathedral, but it is in the country churches that some of the strangest mutants appear. The craftsmen who carved these heads in the fourteenth and fifteenth centuries improvised very freely on the theme, drawing on all the resources of the iconography, not only the frown, the baleful glare, the unfocused eyes but also the tongue sticking out and the fierce teeth (these features, occasionally attributes of leaf demons, but seldom if ever seen in foliate heads of the thirteenth century, became common again in the later Middle Ages). The carvings sometimes reflect limitations of technique but any crudity is more than compensated for by the liveliness and originality of the ideas expressed in the details. At South Tawton, for example, where foliate heads appear on many of the roof bosses, the leafy stem encircling one Green Man's head bifurcates just as it comes out of his mouth, and the short branch is developed as his tongue. The making of Green Man was almost a folk art in these parts, and to observe many variations is like hearing an old folk song sung, not in unison, but by different singers, one after the other, each adding a new verse as he makes it up on the spot.

It is obvious that these Green Men do not all have precisely the same meaning. Some are demons; some probably represent lost souls or sinners. (The leaves coming from the eyes, ears and mouth may sometimes allude to sins committed by these sensory organs – particularly the tongue). Very few of them, however, could be interpreted as the May King, unless perhaps with reference to abuses associated with May Games (?): some of the Green Men look cross-eyed and crapulous and others might well be suffering from a hang-over.

On the fourteenth century sedilia at Weston Longville (Norfolk) two Green Men, one with branches coming out of his mouth, the other with his huge tongue sticking out and his branches growing from the sides of his head, just above his ears, like horns, are placed either side of a little man carrying sprays of foliage – vine and oak. This figure probably represents the Rogationtide processions for the blessing of the fields[59] and the marking of the parish boundaries, when a band of boys carrying green boughs "beat the boundaries". The association of the Rogationtide figure (or, possibly, he is a calendar image: the vines he carries bear grapes, perhaps pointing to September rather than to May?) and the Green Man is probably a decorative association. The two motifs may have no more in common that their leafy sprays.

It can be difficult to distinguish between what is a purely decorative association and what may be a significant association of ideas. Likewise it is often difficult to be sure whether a variation in the image was made for the sake of diversifying the ornament or was intended to give the motif a new twist of meaning. Two very different versions of the Green Man appear in the choir screen in Winchester cathedral: one is represented as an entire figure carrying a sword and buckler (a small round shield used for parrying) and the other is a head in profile with a thick branch held between his teeth. Are these differences wholly explained as decorative variations?

The decorative possibilities of the motif were certainly explored no less imaginatively than its possibilities of meaning. In the Elisabethkirche in Marburg, Lahn, Green Men bloom like exotic flowers among the luxurious leaves of the rood screen. This delightful blossoming is purely decorative. Likewise the remarkably imaginative (and almost imaginary) "Green Man" in the porch of St Mary's, Great Shelford, near Cambridge. It is just, but only just possible to recognise a "face" in the configuration of two large oak leaves. The "mouth" is represented by the space between the proximal leaf lobes and the crossed leaf stalks, and the "nose" by a single acorn. The narrow eye slits appear in the sinuses of the leaf lobes.

Although the Green Man was a much loved motif I think it is very unlikely that he was revered as a symbol of the renewal of life in springtime. The suggestion[60] that the crowned, impish Green Man is the fourteenth century stained glass in a window in St Mary Redcliffe, Bristol, was venerated equally with the Virgin, whose image appears in the same reconstructed window, seems to me highly improbable.

The Green Man's place in the scheme of things may perhaps be better understood from the imagery of the joyous Incarnation group in Exeter Cathedral. The Virgin treads on the Green Man as she might tread on the head of the old serpent, the tempter himself, lurking in the Tree of Life. The leaves rise up out of the wide open mouth as from the abyss: they frame and form the background for the Mother with her smiling Child and the incensing angels hovering above them, but the eye is drawn from the springtime of nature to contemplate the more radiant springtime of grace. I think the association of imagery may well be significant here. The relationship of the Green Man to the Virgin corresponds with his relationship to The Rider in the Bamberg sculpture. He represents the darkness of unredeemed nature as opposed to the shimmering light of Christian revelation.

The dark side of the Green Man's character was never forgotten. He was portrayed as a devil in a carving on a misericord in Chester cathedral, and as an "unclean ape" on a corbel at Langley Marish (Buckinghamshire), and I think it is probable that the Green Men with three faces in one, represented on misericords in Whalley Church and Cartmel Priory respectively, are images of "three-headed Beelzebub", the root of all evil, as at Toscanella. The reappearance of the foliate tricephalos at these two places in north Lancashire and Cumbria in the fifteenth century is most interesting. It is a very rare form of the motif and I know of no other examples in England. There is, however, some evidence that it was perpetuated in Scandinavia, and it has been recorded at Gothem and Vamlingbo in Sweden.[61] The crowned tricephalos at Cartmel is remarkably similar to the head of the figure of Satan represented as *triceps Beelzebub*, the Trinity of Evil, in a miniature in a thirteenth century manuscript in the Bibliothèque Nationale (Paris).[62]

The use of the foliate head on Christian tombs and memorials (a use continued long after the motif had fallen out of favour as an ornament in church architecture) might suggest the idea of resurrection – a life out of death symbol, but could equally well suggest: "For all flesh is as grass and all the glory of man as the flower of grass. The grass withereth and the flower thereof falleth away". Peter 1.24. The Christian soul, having renounced sinful nature – the World, the Flesh and the Devil – at baptism, hoped for salvation through grace after death. A foliate head carved on a font or a tomb could allude to man's fallen and concupiscent nature, or to his brief life on earth – a reminder that "All greenness comes to withering".

The motif was used on the tombs of saints: Sainte-Abre in Poitiers in the fourth and fifth century, and Saint-Étienne in the Cistercian Abbey at Aubazine in the thirteenth century, and St. Frideswide at Oxford. It was used on the tomb of Louis de France, also in the thirteenth century, and on the tomb of a parish priest, William Harrington, at Harpswell in the fourteenth century, and on the Memorial of Abbot Hölein of Ebrach in the seventeenth century. Its use on Memorials was continued into the eighteenth century: a foliate skull appears on the Sandford and Challoner Memorial (*circa* 1741) in St Mary Redcliffe, Bristol. This eighteenth century "Green Man" does not suggest a connection with the eighteenth century Jack in the Green; it is, more likely, a *memento mori*.

The secular use of the foliate head had not yet been extensively studied. It was a popular ornamental motif from the sixteenth century and is still occasionally used as, for example in the panels of the very beautiful stained glass screens by John Piper in the Wessex Hotel, Winchester. These foliate heads were, of course, intended to suggest the roof bosses in the Cathedral, close by.[63] They were, so to speak, caught like echoes from the past, but they are no more copies of medieval carvings that the fourteenth century Green Men are copies of antique leaf masks. They spring into vibrant new life in these wonderful screens, shifting between leaded outlines and colours, changing as they are illuminated both by reflected and transmitted light. The artist has expanded the image. Mr Piper pointed out to me that if one is drawing leaves and branches as a flat, more or less decorative design it seems quite natural to put in two eyes, a nose and a mouth. Surely this explanation accounts for the long continued popularity of the motif. Its various traditional characteristics, the deeply furrowed brow; the baleful glare; the barely focused, sometimes squinting eyes, made it even more exciting. It could not only stimulate but deeply disturb the imagination. It is a dynamic image, capable of infinite expansion. Rarely if ever can the Green Man be considered a "meaningless" ornament or an empty echo. The Green Man whose appearance on the walls of Fountains Abbey in the fifteenth century so sadly anticipated the natural growth of vegetation in the ruins today remains a resonant echo.

The Green Man's story is a long one, with many ramifications and many surprise twists. Much of the story is better told in pictures than in words because we can trace the roots and follow the main growth and the spreading of the branches more easily when the theme is presented visually, but best of all is to seek out and meet the Green Man face to face and let him speak for himself. In following his trail we come to some of the most beautiful places on earth – the churches and cathedrals of the Middle Ages. It is, indeed, a very strange demon that can lead us to such heavenly vistas.

LIST OF REFERENCES

1. LADY RAGLAN
   "The Green Man in Church Architecture"
   Folklore. 50. 1939. pp. 45–57.
2. SIR NIKOLAUS PEVSNER
   The Buildings of England (series)
   Penguin Books.
   (Numerous references to Green Man carvings in the volumes of this series.)
3. C. J. P. CAVE
   "The Roof Bosses in Ely Cathedral"
   Proceedings and Communications. Cambridge Antiquarian Society. 32. 1932. pp. 33–46.
   "Jack in the Green Carvings"
   Letter to *Country Life.* July 4th. 1947. p. 37.
   Roof Bosses in Medieval Churches
   Cambridge University Press. 1948. pp. 65–8.
4. GEOFFREY GRIGSON
   The Englishman's Flora
   Jarrold and Son. Norwich. 1960. (p. 114; p. 168; pp. 251–2.)
   The Shell Country Alphabet. 1966. (pp. 183–4. Illustration. p. 167.)
   Looking and Finding
   Carousel Books. 1971. (pp. 55–6.)
5. C. J. P. CAVE. 1932. *loc. cit.*
6. FRITZ SAXL
   A Heritage of Images
   Penguin Books. 1970.
7. W. H. ST. JOHN HOPE
   "Fountains Abbey, Yorkshire"
   Yorkshire Archaeological Journal. 15. 1296.

   Pp. 27–8: "Owing to an unequal settlement of the foundations of the gables, the masonry has been dislocated in parts; in two places, to such an extent as to seriously misplace the arches of the window heads. To make good the disruption, Abbot Darnton inserted in one window, the northernmost on the east side, a new stone, elaborately carved; on the outside with a head amongst the foliage issuing from the mouth, on the inside with a rose and an angel carrying a scroll and dated *Anno Domini* 1483."
8. MAX WEGNER
   "Blattmasken"
   Das siebente Jahrzehnt. Festschrift zum 70. Geburtstag von Adolph Goldschmidt. Berlin. 1935. pp. 43–50.
9. HARALD KELLER
   "Blattmaske"
   Reallexikon zur deutschen Kunstgeschichte. 2. Stuttgart. 1948. pp. 867–74.
10. J. M. C. TOYNBEE AND J. B. WARD PERKINS
    "Peopled Scrolls: A Hellenistic Motif in Imperial Art"
    Papers of the British School at Rome. 18. 1950. pp. 1–43.
11. THEODOR WIEGAND
    Baalbek
    Berlin and Leipzig. 1921–5.
12. OTTO PUCHSTEIN AND THEODOR LEUPKE
    Ba'albek
    Berlin. 1905.
13. LOUIS VALENSI
    Présentation d'Oeuvres Gallo-Romaines
    Musée d'Aquitaine. 1964–65.
14. NELSON GLUECK
    Deities and Dolphins: the story of the Naboteans
    Cassell. 1966.
15. J. M. C. TOYNBEE
    Art in Roman Britian
    Phaidon Press. London. 1962.
16. J. M. C. TOYNBEE
    Art in Britain under the Romans
    London. 1964.
17. J. M. C. TOYNBEE. 1962. *loc. cit.*
18. WILHELM VON MASSOW
    Die Grabmäler von Neumagen
    Berlin and Leipzig. 1932.
19. HAROLD KELLER. 1948. *loc. cit.*
20. WILHELM VON MASSOW. 1932. *loc. cit.*
21. J. M. C. TOYNBEE (Personal communication.)
22. O. NAVARRE
    "Persona"
    Dictionnaire des Antiquités grecques et romaines. 1877.
    C. Daremberg; E. Saglio; E. Pottier. 4. p. 406
23. J. N. VON WILMOWSKY
    Der Dom zu Trier
    Trier. 1874.
24. EUGEN VON MERCKLIN
    Antike Figuralkapitelle
    Deutsches Archäologisches Institut. Berlin. 1962. pp. 135–40: "Blattmasken".
25. NIKOLAUS IRSCH
    Die Kunstdenkmäler der Rheinprovinz: Der dom zu Trier. Dusseldorf. 1931.
26. THEODOR KONRAD KEMPF
    "Untersuchungen und Beobachtungen am Trierer Dom, 1961–63"
    Germania. 42. pp. 126–41.
27. ERICH GOSE
    "Der Tempel am Herrenbrünnchen in Trier"
    Trier Zeitschrift für Geschichte und Kunst des Trierer Landes und seiner Nachbargebiete. 30. Jahrgang 1967. pp. 82–100.
28. EDITH MARY WIGHTMAN
    Roman Trier and the Treveri
    Rupert Hart-Davis. London. 1970.
29. EDMOND LE BLANT

Les sarcophages chrétiens de la Gaule
Paris. 1886. p. 85.

30.   H. LECLERQ
       Dictionnaire d'archéologie chrétienne et liturgie. 14. col.
       1315 and 1335.
       1939.

31.   GUSTAVE MENDEL
       *Musées imperiaux ottomans: Catalogue des sculptures
       grècques, romaines et byzantines.* 2. 1912–14. pp. 546–9.

32.   JOHN BECKWITH
       Early Medieval Art
       Thames and Hudson. London. 1964.

33.   *M. S. Cod. sanct,* 6; Cod. Gertrudianus. fol. 17. (*circa*
       983)
       Museo Archeologico Nazionale. Cividale.

34.   *M. S. Codex Egberti. fol.* 2v. (*circa* 985)
       Stadtbibliothek. Trier.

35.   RABANUS MAURUS. (784 to 856). Abbot of Fulda
       and Archbishop of Mainz
       Patrologia Latina. 112. col. 1037
       edited: J. P. Migne. Paris. 1878–90.
           "Ramus voluptas carnis, ut in Ezechiele: Ecce ap-
       plicant ramum ad nares suos", quod reprobi in vol-
       untate carnis delectantur. . . . Per ramos homines
       pravi, ut in Job: "Ramos ejus arefaciet flamma, quod
       pravos vastabit damnatio aeterna."

36.   R. PETTAZZONI
       "The Pagan origin of the three-headed representation
       of the Christian Trinity"
       Journal of the Warburg and Courtauld Institutes. 9.
       1946. pp. 135–51.

37.   WILLIBALD KIRFEL
       Die Dreiköpfige Gottheit
       Bonn. 1948. (pp. 148–73: "Die dreiköpfigen und drei-
       gesichtigen Gestalten des christlichen Mittelalters".)

38.   CONSTANTINUS DE TISCHENDORF
       Evanglia apocrypha, Lipsiae, 1876. p. 400.

39.   FERDINAND PIPER
       Mythologie der christlichen Kunst. I.
       Weimar, 1847. pp. 404ff.

40.   E. HENNECKE AND W. SCHNEEMELCHER
       Neutestamentliche Apokryphen I
       Tübingen. 1959. p. 351.

41.   HERBERT SCHADE
       *Dämonen und Monstren: Gestaltungen des Bösen in
       der Kunst des frühen Mittelalters*
       Verlag Friedrich Pustet. Regensburg. 1962. (pp. 43, 44).

42.   Folkunge Psalter. MS Thott 143, 2°. f. 17v.
       Royal Library. Copenhagen.

43.   ST. BERNARD OF CLAIRVAUX
       Apologia ad Wilhelmum
       Patrologia Latina. 182. col. 914.

44.   CHARLES E. KEYSER
       A List of Norman Tympana and Lintels
       1904.

45.   GEORG ZARNECKI
       Later English Romanesque Sculpture
       Tiranti. London. 1953.

46.   HERBERT SCHADE. *loc. cit.* p. 64 and note 196.

47.   A. GRABAR AND C. NORDENFALK
       Romanesque Painting
       Skira, New York. 1958
           P. 159. (illustration): Tree of Good and Evil. (Arbor
       bona-Arbor mala) in LIBER FLORIDUS. St. Omer,
       before 1120. Cod. 1125, folios 231 verso and 232. Bib-
       liothèque de l'Université, Ghent.

48.   JEAN ADHÉMAR
       "La Fontaine de Saint Denis"
       Revue Archéologique. I. (1936). pp. 224–32.

49.   RICHARD H. L. HAMANN-MACLEAN
       "Antikenstudium in der Kunst des Mittelalters"
       Marburger Jahrbuch für Kunstwissenschaft. 15. pp. 157–
       250. 1949–50. (Plates 119, 120.)

50.   HANS R. HAHNLOSER
       Villard de Honnecourt
       Vienna. 1935. (Plate 10, *a* and *b*; plate 43, *c* and *d*)

51.   HARALD KELLER. *loc. cit.*

52.   LOTTLISA BEHLING
       Die Pflanzenwelt der Mittelalterlichen Kathedralen
       Cologne. 1964.

53.   Quotation from poem "Long life, O Man, you hope
       to gain"
       No. 29. p. 64 in *Medieval English Verse,* translated by
       Brian Stone.
       Penguin Books. 1964.

54.   SIR NIKOLAUS PEVSNER
       The Leaves of Southwell
       King Penguin Books. 1945.

55.   A. C. SEWARD
       "The foliage, flowers and fruit of Southwell Chapter
       House"
       Proceedings of the Cambridge Antiquarian Society. vol.
       35. pp. 1–32. 1933–34.

56.   CHRISTINA HOLE
       English Custom and Usage
       Batsford. London (3rd edition). 1950. plate 52.

57.   ROY JUDGE. Personal communication.

58.   Quotation from "Piranesi's Prison Etchings" by Her-
       man Melville.

59.   M. D. ANDERSON
       Introductory essay on the iconography of misericords
       in the *Catalogue of Misericords in Great Britain,* by
       G. L. Remnant, Oxford. 1969.

60.   LADY RAGLAN. *loc. cit.* p. 56.

61.   ASGER JORN AND NOëL ARNAUD
       La langue verte et la cuite. Paris. 1968. (Plates 276 and
       285.)

62.   MS. latin 11560 5v°.

63.   JOHN PIPER. (Personal Communication.)

PLATES

PLATE 1
TRIER. RHEINISCHES LANDESMUSEUM. Cast taken from a leaf mask on one of the
capitals walled up in Trier Cathedral. The capitals, salvaged by Bishop Nicetius from the ruins
in a Roman temple in Trier (*Am Herrenbrünnchen*), dating from the first half of the 2nd
century A.D., were remounted on pillars set up at the corners of the Square Chancel when it
was restored in the 6th century.

PLATE 2a
BAALBEK, LEBANON. Leaf mask in a frieze on the Bacchus Temple build during the time of Antonius Pius (138–161 A.D.) (*Photo. British Library.*)

PLATE 2b
HATRA, MESOPOTAMIA. (AL HADR, IRAQ). Male Medusa on the façade of a temple dating from the mid-2nd century A.D. (*Photo. Professor J. B. Ward-Perkins.*)

PLATE 3a

TRIER. RHEINISCHES LANDESMUSEUM. Leaf mask, probably representing Okeanos, on a reconstructed fragment from a funerary monument. Neumagen. 2nd or 3rd century A.D.

PLATE 3b

TRIER. RHEINISCHES LANDESMUSEUM. Leaf mask in the centre of a panel from the Iphigneienpfeiler. Neumagen. 2nd or 3rd century A.D.

PLATE 4a
TRIER. RHEINISCHES LANDESMUSEUM. Leaf masks in a frieze. Fragment from a funerary
monument. Neumagen. 2nd or 3rd century A.D.

PLATE 4b
TRIER. RHEINISCHES LANDESMUSEUM. Two faces formed from acanthus. Schulreliefpfeiler.
Neumagen. 2nd or 3rd century A.D.

PLATE 5a
ÉVREUX (Eure). MUSÉE MUNICIPALE D'ÉVREUX. Capital. 3rd century A.D.

PLATE 5b
BORDEAUX (Gironde). MUSÉE D'AQUITAINE. Gallo-Roman frieze. (*Foto-Marburg*)

PLATE 6a
ISTANBUL. ARCHAEOLOGICAL MUSEUM. Capital with leaf masks and horns of plenty. 6th century.

PLATE 6b
ISTANBUL. ARCHAEOLOGICAL MUSEUM. Capital (opposite face).

PLATE 7
ISTANBUL. ARCHAEOLOGICAL MUSEUM. Capital. 6th century. Leaf masks with a horn of
plenty between them.

PLATE 8a
ISTANBUL. ARCHAEOLOGICAL MUSEUM. Capital. 6th century.

PLATE 8b
ISTANBUL. ARCHAEOLOGICAL MUSEUM. Capital (adjacent face).

PLATE 9a
ISTANBUL. ARCHAEOLOGICAL MUSEUM. Capital with squinting leaf mask. 6th century.

PLATE 9b
ISTANBUL. ARCHAEOLOGICAL MUSEUM. Capital. 6th century.

PLATE 10
ISTANBUL. ARCHAEOLOGICAL MUSEUM. Capital. 6th century.

PLATE 11
POITIERS (Vienne). SAINT-HILAIRE-LE-GRAND. Tomb of Sainte-Abre (base of the lid).
4th or 5th century.

PLATE 12
PARIS. MUSÉE DES MONUMENTS FRANÇAIS. Cast from capital in the crypt of Dijon
Cathedral. 9th century.

PLATE 13
CIVIDALE DEL FRIULI. MUSEO ARCHEOLOGICO NAZIONALE. Dedication page of
Egbert's Psalter. *circa* 980. (*Photo. Museo Archeologico Nazionale, Cividale del Friuli*)

PLATE 14
TRIER, STADTBIBLIOTHEK. Dedication page of Codex Egberti. *circa* 980. (*Foto-Marburg*)

PLATE 15
TOSCANELLA. SAN PIETRO. Façade. 12th century. (*Photo: Alinari-Giraudon, Paris*)

PLATE 16a
REIMS (Marne). MUSÉE RÉMI. Gallo-Roman tricephalos.

PLATE 16b
AVIGNON (Vaucluse). MUSÉE CALVET. Capital. 12th century. (*Foto-Marburg*)

xpi pstant innumera beneficia. & in
demoniacis aliusq; infirmis patrocinan
tib; eisde martyrib; diuina fiunt mi
racula. ut omib; liqdo patefiat quanta
merta martyru eox apud diuina cle
mentia existat. Intectis de hinc aliqt
annox curriculis. beati oorooxii corpus
ad romana urbe transfert. postuuq; ua
latina int duas lauros honorabilit &
glose uenerat. Magnu quippe inscis
martyrib; suis fidelib; xpe patrociniu
pparauit. qui post ingressu utrx; etne
corpora eox diuisit ut unus pa ti troci
et grecie alter sce romane eccle. S; licet

Incip passio. scox martyru Felicis & Regule

vlt qx is
numerabi
liuq; por be
pciosa ex
titit inc
spectu dni
mors scox
ex. qui pro
cruore
fideq; in
tegerrima

ecclam plantauert. Exquib; n minima
... rnarib; maximianu crudelissimi

PLATE 17a
STUTTGART. WÜRTTEMBERGISCHES LANDESBIBLIOTHEK. Initial. Passional.
12th century. (*Foto-Marburg*)

PLATE 17b
AUTUN (Saône-et-Loire). CATHEDRAL. Capital. 12th century. (*Foto-Marburg*)

PLATE 18a, b, c
CASTOR, Huntingdon and Peterborough. St. KYNEBURGA. Capitals. 12th century.

PLATE 19a
MARS (Nièvre). Tympanum. 12th century. (*Foto-Marburg*)

PLATE 19*b*
COPENHAGEN. THE ROYAL LIBRARY. Beatus Initial of Folkunge Psalter. 12th century.
(*Photo. Det Kongelige Bibliotek, Copenhagen*)

PLATE 20a
EIKSTONE, Gloucestershire. ST. JOHN THE EVANGELIST. Tympanum. 12th century.

PLATE 20b
LINLEY. Shropshire. ST. LEONARD. Tympanum. 12th century.

PLATE 21a
CHATEAUNEUF-sur-CHARENTE (Charente). SAINT-PIERRE. Capital. 12th century.
(*Foto-Marburg*)

PLATE 21b
KÖNIGSLUTTER am ELM (former Abbey Church). Corbel. 12th century. (*Foto-Marburg*)

PLATE 22
KILPECK, Herefordshire. St. MARY and St. David. Doorway. 12th century.

PLATE 23a
SAINT-DENIS (Seine). DEPôT LAPIDAIRE DE L'ABBAYE. Fountain. *circa* 1200.

PLATE 23b
Head of Silvanus of the basin of the fountain.

PLATE 24*a*
CHARTRES (Eure-et-Loir). CATHEDRAL. Foliate heads above the portal of the south transept.
13th century.

PLATE 24*b*
REIMS (Marne). CATHEDRAL. Leaf masks on the inner west wall. 13th century.

PLATE 25a
POITIERS (Vienne). CATHEDRAL. Misericord carving. 13th century.

PLATE 25b
SEMUR en AUXOIS (Côte d'Or). NOTRE-DAME. Corbel. 13th century.

PLATE 26a
POITIERS (Vienne). CATHEDRAL. Spandrel in the choir screen. 13th century.

PLATE 26b
AUBAZINE (Corrèze). Abbey. Leaf mask on the base of the tomb of Saint Étienne d'Aubazine. 13th century.

PLATE 27
AUXERRE (Yonne.) CATHEDRAL. *Tête de Feuilles* above a capital. 13th century.

PLATE 28
AUXERRE (Yonne). CATHEDRAL. *Têtes de Feuilles* above a capital. 13th century.

PLATE 29*a*
AUXERRE (Yonne) CATHEDRAL. Crowned head with foliate moustache. 13th century.

PLATE 29 *b* and *c*
MONTIER-en-DER (Haute Marne). NOTRE DAME. Roof Bosses 13th century. (*Foto Marburg*)

PLATE 30a
TROYES (Aube). SAINT URBAIN. Leaf demon on lintel. 13th century.

PLATE 30b
SEMUR-en-AUXIOS (Côte d'Or). NOTRE DAME. *Masques Feuillus*. 13th century.

PLATE 31 *a* and *b*
PARIS. MUSÉE DES MONUMENTS FRANÇAIS. Foliate head at the base of the tomb of Louis de France.
13th century.

PLATE 31*c*
PARIS. MUSÉE DE CLUNY. Harness ornament. 13th century.

PLATES 32*a* and *b*
NOYON (Oise) CATHEDRAL. Roof bosses in the Chapter House. 13th century.

PLATE 33a
MAINZ CATHEDRAL. Tympanum over the Market Portal. 1200-15.

PLATE 33b
Detail: one of the leaf masks in the border.

PLATE 34a
WORMS CATHDRAL. Tympanum 1200. (*Foto Marburg*).

PLATE 34b
MARIA LAACH ABBEY. Capital *circa* 1230.

PLATE 35
ASCHAFFENBURG. ST. PETER and ST. ALEXANDER. Corbel 1220.

PLATE 36
GELNHAUSEN. MARIENKIRCHE. Head of leaves. *circa* 1235.

PLATE 37
BAMBERG CATHEDRAL. The Rider Statue with an acanthus mask on the console. *circa* 1237.
(*Foto-Limmer*)

PLATE 38
BAMBERG CATHEDRAL. The acanthus leaf mask. (*Foto-Limmer*)

PLATE 39
EBRACH (former Abbey) Leaf masks on the portal. 13th century.
(*a*) Keystone (*b*) boss.

PLATE 40
FRIEDBURG. LIEBFRAUENKIRCHE. Tympanum. *circa* 1290.
(*Foto-Marburg*)

PLATE 41a
MAINZ ALTERTUMSMUSEUM. Roof Boss. Late 13th or early 14th century. (*Foto Marburg*)

PLATE 41b
WÜRZBURG DEUTSCHAUSKIRCHE. Roof boss. *circa* 1290.

PLATE 42*a* and *b*
MUCH MARCLE, Herefordshire. ST. BARTHOLOMEW. Capitals *circa* 1230-40.

PLATE 43*a*
WADENHOE, Northamptonshire. ST. MARY. Corbel 13th century.

PLATE 43*b*
GRANTHAM, Lincolnshire. ST. WULFRAM. Corbel 13th century.

PLATE 44*a*
RIPON, Yorkshire. CATHEDRAL. Corbel 13th century.

PLATE 44*b*
DORCHESTER, Oxfordshire, ABBEY. Corbel, 13th century.

PLATE 45a, b, c, and d
SOUTHWELL, Nottinghamshire, MINSTER. Tympana in the Chapter House. Late 13th Century.

PLATE 46a, b, c, and d
SOUTHWELL. Tympana.

PLATE 47a
SOUTHWELL, Hawthorn mask.

PLATE 47b
CADNEY, Lincolnshire. ALL SAINTS. Corbel 13th century

PLATE 47c
SOUTHWELL, Corbel.

PLATE 48a
NOYON (Oise) CATHEDRAL. Green Man with vines and birds. 13th century.

PLATE 48b
SUTTON BENGER, Wiltshire. ALL SAINTS. Green Man with hawthorn and birds. ? early 14th century.

PLATE 49
EXETER, Devon. CATHEDRAL. Corbel. Late 13th or early 14th century.

PLATE 50a and b
EXETER CATHEDRAL. Roof bosses. Early 14th century.

PLATE 51a
HALSE, Somerset. ST. JAMES. Roundel. *circa* 1300.

PLATE 51b
CLAYPOLE, Lincolnshire. ST. PETER. Capital *circa* 1325.

PLATE 52*a* and *b*
HARPSWELL, Lincolnshire, ST. CHAD. Memorial of William Harrington, rector. +1350.

PLATE 53
WINCHESTER, Hampshire, CATHEDRAL. Spandrel in choir stalls, early 14th century.

PLATE 54
WINCHESTER CATHEDRAL. Spandrel in choir stalls.

PLATE 55a
BEVERLEY, Yorkshire, MINSTER. Capital. 14th century.

PLATE 55b
LICHFIELD, Staffordshire, CATHEDRAL. Capital 1340.

PLATE 56
LECKHAMPSTEAD, Buckinghamshire. Panel on font. 14th century.

PLATE 57*a* and *b*
ELY, Cambridgeshire, CATHEDRAL. Roof bosses in the Lady Chapel, 1335-53.

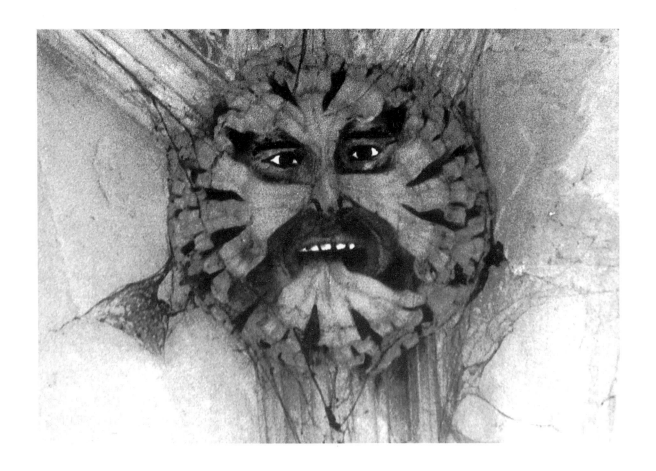

PLATE 58 *a* and *b*
ELY CATHEDRAL. Roof Bosses.

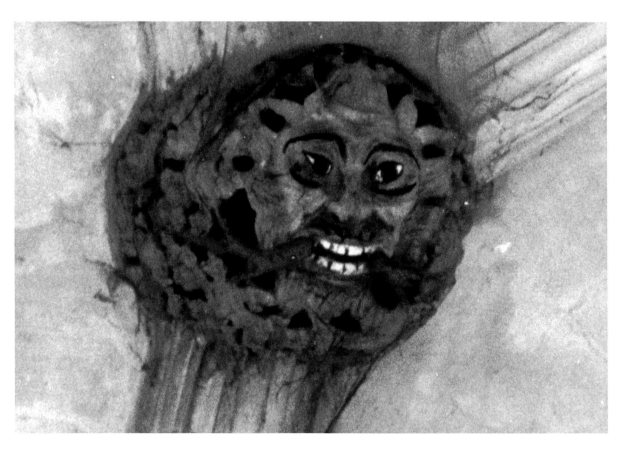

PLATE 59a and b
ELY CATHEDRAL. Roof bosses.

PLATE 60*a* and *b*
ELY CATHEDRAL. Roof bosses.

PLATE 61
MARBURG an der LAHN. ELISABETHKIRCHE.
Rood Screen ? *circa* 1349. (*Foto Marburg*)

PLATE 62a
MARBURG/LAHN. Rood screen with many faces in the leaves. (*Foto Marburg*)

PLATE 62b
MARBURG/LAHN. One of the faces in the Rood Screen. (*Foto Marburg*)

PLATE 63*a*, *b*, and *c*
WESTON LONGVILLE, Norfolk, ALL SAINTS.
Figures at the springing of the arches of the sedilia. 14th century.

PLATE 64a
BRISTOL. ST. MARY REDCLIFFE. Corbel. 14th century.

PLATE 64b
BRISTOL. ST. MARY REDCLIFFE. Roof boss. 14th century.

PLATE 65a
BRISTOL. ST. MARY REDCLIFFE. Green Man in stained glass. 14th century.

PLATE 65b
SOUTHWELL, Nottinghamshire, MINSTER. Misericord. 14th century.

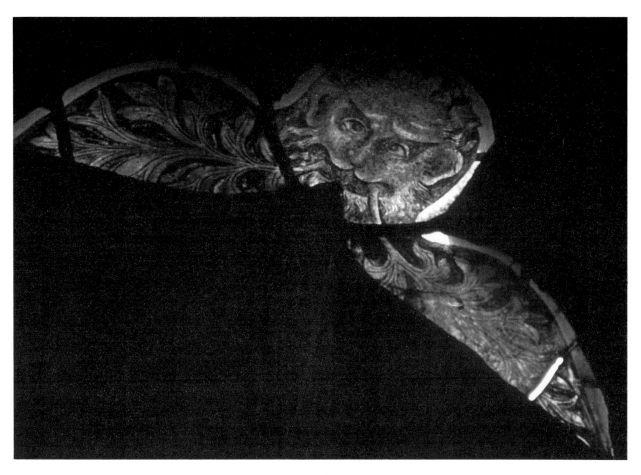

PLATE 66a
NANTWICH, Cheshire, ST. MARY. Stained glass. 14th century.

PLATE 66b
NANTWICH. ST. MARY. Sandstone head. 14th century.

PLATE 67a
COVENTRY, Warwickshire, HOLY TRINITY. Misericord. Late 14th or early 15th century.

PLATE 67b
LOVERSALL, Yorkshire, ST. KATHERINE. Misericord. Late 14th or early 15th century.

PLATE 68
LINCOLN CATHEDRAL. Choir stalls, late 14th century. (a) Misericord (b) Armrest.

PLATE 69
BAMBERG CATHEDRAL. Foliate head in choir stalls. Late 14th century (*Foto Marburg*)

PLATE 70a
CHESTER CATHEDRAL. Misericord. 1390.

PLATE 70b
MARBURG/LAHN. UNIVERSITÄTSMUSEUM. Roof boss. 14th century. (*Foto Marburg*)

PLATE 71 *a* and *b*
SOUTH TAWTON, Devon. ST. ANDREW. Roof bosses 14th or 15th century.

PLATE 72a and b
SOUTH TAWTON. ST. ANDREW. Roof bosses, 14th or 15th century.

PLATE 73*a* and *b*
SAMPFORD COURTENAY, Devon. ST. ANDREW. Roof bosses 14th or 15th century

PLATE 74a
SAMPFORD COURTENAY. ST. ANDREW. Roof boss. 14th or 15th century.

PLATE 74b
SPREYTON, Devon. ST. MICHAEL. Roof boss. 14th or 15th century.

PLATE 75*a*
MELROSE, Roxburgh, Scotland. Abbey Museum. Roof boss. 15th century.

PLATE 75*b*
OTTERY ST. MARY. Devon. ST MARY. Corbel. 14th century.

PLATE 76
LOSTWITHIEL, Cornwall. ST. BARTHOLOMEW. Font. 14th or 15th century.

PLATE 77 *a* and *b*
NORWICH CATHEDRAL. Roof bosses in the Cloisters. 14th or 15th century.

PLATE 78 *a* and *b*
NORWICH CATHEDRAL. Roof bosses in the Cloisters. 14th or 15th century.

PLATE 79 *a* and *b*
NORWICH CATHEDRAL. Roof bosses in the Cloisters. 14th or 15th century.

PLATE 80 *a* and *b*
NORWICH CATHEDRAL. Roof bosses in the Cloisters. 14th or 15th century.

PLATE 81 *a* and *b*
LANGLEY MARISH, Buckinghamshire, ST. MARY. Corbels. 15th century.

PLATE 82a
MILDENHALL, Suffolk. ST. MARY. Boss inside the porch. 15th century.

PLATE 82b
GREAT SHELFORD, Cambridgeshire, ST. MARY. Boss inside the porch. 15th century.

PLATE 83a
WHALLEY, Lancashire, ST. MARY and ALL SAINTS. Misericord. 15th century. Foliate tricephalos.

PLATE 83b
WHALLEY, Lancashire. ST. MARY and ALL SAINTS. Misericord. 15th century. Foliate head.

PLATE 84*a*
CUMBRIA, Lancashire. PRIORY. Misericord. 15th century. Crowned foliate tricephalos.

PLATE 84*b*
PARIS. BIBLIOTHÈQUE NATIONALE. Miniature in a 13th century MS. Satan as *triceps*
Beelzebub, the Trinity of Evil. (*Photo. Bibliothèque Nationale*)

PLATE 85a
KINGS LYNN, Norfolk. ST. MARGARET. Misericord. 14th century. Cross-eyed Green Man.

PLATE 85b
LUDLOW, Shropshire, ST. LAURENCE. Misericord. 16th century. Cross-eyed Green men as supporters.

PLATE 86a
LLANGWM, Monmouthshire (Gwent). ST. JEROME. Corbel. Probably 15th century.

PLATE 86b
LLANTILIO CROSSENNY, Monmouthshire (Gwent). ST. TEILO. Carving on the wall in north transept.
14th or 15th century.

PLATE 87a
CROWLAND, Lincolnshire, ABBEY. Roof boss. 15th century.

PLATE 87b
QUEEN CAMEL, Somerset. ST. BARNABAS. Roof boss. Probably 15th century.

PLATE 88
WHALLEY, Lancashire, ST. MARY and ALL SAINTS. Canopy in the choir stalls. ? 15th century.

PLATE 89
ASTBURY, Cheshire. ST. MARY. Roof boss. 15th century.

PLATE 90a
SILKSTONE, Yorkshire, ALL SAINTS. Roof boss. 15th century.

PLATE 90b
NORWICH CATHEDRAL. Misericord. Late 15th century.

PLATE 91
BISHOPS LYDEARD, Somerset. ST MARY. Bench end. 15th century.

PLATE 92
CROWCOMBE, Somerset. HOLY GHOST. Bench end. 16th century.

PLATE 93a
HEREFORD CATHEDRAL. Lintel carving. 15th century

PLATE 93*b*
BOSBURY, Herefordshire, HOLY TRINITY. Monument to Richard Harford and his wife. 16th century.
One of two Green men.

PLATE 94

EBRACH (Former Cistertian Abbey). Leaf mask at the base of the Memorial of Abbot Hölein. 17th century.

PLATE 95
BRISTOL. ST. MARY. REDCLIFFE. Foliate skull at the base of the Sandford and Challoner Memorial.
(La. Paty. Bristol, fecit), *circa* 1747.

LIST OF PLATES

1. *Trier. Rheinisches Landesmuseum*
    Cast taken from one of the capitals dating from the first half of the 2nd century A.D., discovered by J. N. von Wilmowsky during excavations in Trier Cathedral *circa* 1874. The capitals, salvaged from the ruins of a Roman temple (*Am Herrenbrünnchen*) of the Hadrianic period (117–138 A.D.) by Bishop Nicetius, were remounted on pillars set up at the corners of the Square Chancel when it was restored in the 6th century. The pillars were finally hidden from view when this part of the cathedral was again restored and partly rebuilt between 1028 and 1037.

2. (a) *Baalbek, Lebanon. Bacchus Temple*
    Leaf mask in a frieze on a temple built in the time of Antoninus Pius (138–161 A.D.). (*Photo. British Library.*)
    (b) *Hatra, Mesopotamia. (Al Hadr, Iraq)*
    Male Medusa on the façade of a temple dating from the mid-second century A.D. (*Photo. Professor J. B. Ward Perkins.*)

3. (a) *Trier, Rheinisches Landesmuseum*
    Leaf mask, probably representing Okeanos, on a reconstructed fragment from a funerary monument. Neumagen. 2nd or 3rd century A.D.
    (b) *Trier, Rheinisches Landesmuseum*
    Leaf mask in the centre of a panel from the Iphigenien-pfeiler. Neumagen. 2nd or 3rd century A.D.

4. (a) *Trier, Rheinisches Landesmuseum*
    Leaf masks in a frieze. Fragment from a funerary monument. Neumagen. 2nd or 3rd century A.D.
    (b) *Trier, Rheinisches Landesmuseum*
    Two faces formed from acanthus in a fragment of a frieze from the Schulreliefpfeiler. Neumagen. 2nd or 3rd century A.D.

5. (a) *Évreux (Eure) Musée Municipale*
    Leaf mask on a Roman capital. 3rd century.
    Leaves sprout from all parts of the face and from the corners of the mouth; even the eyes are formed from rolled up leaves.
    (b) Bordeaux (Gironde). Musée d'Aquitaine
    Faces formed from leaves in Gallo-Roman frieze. (*Bildarchiv Foto-Marburg: No. LA 632/27.*)

6. *Istanbul. Archaeological Museum*
    (a) Capital discovered in the City Wall during excavations, 1972. (Museum No. 7237). 6th century. Leaf mask with horns of plenty.
    (b) Another leaf mask on the same capital (opposite face).

7. *Istanbul. Archaeological Museum*
    Capital discovered at Mudanya in 1885. (Museum No. 748). 6th century.
    Two leaf masks with a horn of plenty between them.

8. *Istanbul. Archaeological Museum*
    Capital with a leaf mask on each of its four faces. (Museum No. 749). 6th century.
    (a) The pupils of the eyes converge slightly, and the large irises are raised, almost bulging, giving the face an intense "far away" expression.
    (b) Adjacent face. The mask has similar prominent and barely focused eyes.

9. *Istanbul. Archaeological Museum*
    Capitals discovered *circa* 1953 on the site of the New Palace of Justice, Istanbul. 6th century.
    (a) (Museum No. not recorded). The eyes squint.
    (b) (Museum No. 5073A).

10. *Istanbul. Archaeological Museum*
    Capital discovered *circa* 1972–73 at Kanlica. 6th century. (Museum No. 5977).

11. *Poitiers (Vienne). Saint-Hilaire-le-Grand*
    Carving on the base of the lid of the tomb of Sainte-Abre. 4th or 5th century.
    Sainte Abre was the daughter of St Hilary the Great. She died *circa* 361.

12. *Paris. Musée des Monuments Français*
    Cast of a capital in the crypt of the cathedral in Dijon (Côte d'Or). 9th century.

13. *Cividale de Friuli. Museo Archeologico Nazionale.*
    Dedication page of the Psalter presented to Archbishop Egbert of Trier in 983.
    MS Cod. sanct. 6; Cod. Gertrudianus fol. 17.

14. *Trier. Stadtbibliothek*
    Dedication page of the *Codes Egberti, fol. 2. vs.* presented to Archbishop Egbert in 985. (*Bildarchiv Foto-Marburg No. 59662.*)

15. *Toscanella. Façade of San Pietro*
    Two demons, each in the form of a tricephalos; probably representing *triceps Beelzebub*, 12th century. (*Photo. Alinari-Giraudon, Paris. No. 26150.*)

16. (a) *Reims (Marne). Musée Rémi*
    Gallo-Roman tricephalos
    (b) *Avignon (Vaucluse). Musée Calvet*
    Capital (from Notre-Dame, Avignon). 12th century. (*Bildarchiv Foto-Marburg No. 23030.*)

17. (a) *Stuttgart. Württembergisches Landesbibliothek*
    Codex. bibl. 2: 56. Stuttgarter Passionale II. fol. 83v. Initial M in the form of a demon with monsters coming from the ears and tendrils coming out of the mouth. (*Bildarchiv Foto-Marburg No. LA 2211/1.*)
    (b) *Autun (Saône-et-Loire)*
    Capital in the cathedral (Saint-Lazare). 12th century. Man-Eating leaf demon. (*Bildarchiv Foto-Marburg No. 31726.*)

18. *Castor (Near Peterborough). St. Kyneburga*
    Capital dated 1124.

(a) Mask with tendrils coming from the mouth.
(b) Mask with tendrils coming from the nose.
(c) Cat mask, with human hands holding the branches that come from the mouth.

19.   (a) *Mars (Nièvre)*
Tympanum. 12th century. (*Bildarchiv Foto-Marburg No. 39880.*)
(b) *Copenhagen. The Royal Library. (Det Kongelige Bibliotek.)*
f. 17 of the Folkunge Psalter MS Thott 143, fol. 2. 12th century.
Beatus Initial. (*Photo. Detkongelige Bibliotek. Copenhagen.*)

20.   (a) *Elkstone, Gloucestershire. St. John the Evangelist*
Tympanum. *circa* 1160.
Mask with tendrils coming out of the mouth (in right hand corner of the tympanum).
(b) *Linley, Shropshire. St. Leonard*
Tympanum. *circa* 1138.
Nude figure surrounded by foliage. Sprays of foliage come from the mouth.

21.   (a) *Châteauneuf-sur-Charente (Charente). Saint-Pierre*
Capital. 12th century.
Foliate beasts with man holding their tongues. (*Bildarchiv Foto-Marburg. No. 38688.*)
(b) *Königslutter am Elm (former Abbey Church)*
Corbel on the principal apse. *circa* 1135.
Foliate head of a type rarely seen in 12th century art. Leaves grow on the face, forming the whiskers, beard and moustache, and the expression is deeply serious. It bears a close resemblance to the leaf masks of antiquity. (*Bildarchiv Foto-Marburg. No. 12332.*)

22.   *Kilpeck. Herefordshire. St. Mary and St. David*
Doorway (leaf mask on abacus on right). *circa* 1140.

23.   *Saint-Denis (Seine). Depôt Lapidaire de l'Abbaye*
(a) Fountain from the cloisters of the abbey, *circa* 1200. The basin is decorated with the heads of Roman gods, each one has the name inscribed above it.
(b) Head of Silvanus in the form of a leaf mask.

24.   (a) *Chartres (Eure-et-Loir). Cathedral*
Three foliate heads above the portal of the south transept. 13th century.
The head in the centre is in the form of a *Tête de Feuilles*; the heads of either side are *Masques Feuillus*: the one on the right has sprays of oak coming out of the mouth, the one on the left has vines.
(b) *Reims (Marne). Cathedral*
Inner west wall. 13th century.
Two leaf masks, very similar to one example of the *Tête de Feuilles* illustrated by Villard de Honnecourt, 1235.

25.   (a) *Poitiers (Vienne). Cathedral*
Misericord carving. 13th century
(b) *Semur-en-Auxois. (Côte d'Or). Notre-Dame*
Corbel. 13th century.

26.   (a) *Poitiers (Vienne). Cathedral*
Leaf mask filling a spandrel in the choir screen. 13th century.
(b) *Aubazine (Corrèze). Abbey*
Leaf mask on the tomb of Saint-Etienne, d'Aubazine †1154. 13th century.
The Abbey at Aubazine was built by the Cistercians

in the 12th century.

27.   *Auxerre (Yonne). Cathedral*
Tête de Feuilles. A head of fluttering leaves. 13th century.

28.   *Auxerre (Yonne). Cathedral*
Tête de Feuilles above abacus of capital with vine leaves and grapes. 13th century.

29.   (a) *Auxerre (Yonne). Cathedral*
Crowned head with foliate moustache. 13th century.
(b) *Montier-en-Der (Haute Marne). Notre Dame*
Roof boss. 13th century.
Tête de Feuilles, with some foliage coming from the mouth. (*Bildarchiv Foto-Marburg. No. LA 1372/25.*)
(c) *Montier-en-Der (Haute Marne). Notre Dame*
Roof boss. 13th century.
Tête de Feuilles, with foliage coming from the nose and developing from the lips at each side of the mouth. (*Bildarchiv Foto-Marburg. No. LA 1372/28.*)

30.   (a) *Troyes (Aube). Saint-Urbain*
Lintel over portal. 13th century.
Leaf demon with horns. A *Masque Feuillu.* The sprays of leaves coming from the mouth extend to fill the lower and right hand border.
(b) *Semur-en-Auxois (Côte d'Or). Notre Dame*
Masques Feuillus with vines. 13th century.

31.   (a) *Paris. Musée des Monuments Français*
Tête de Feuilles on the base of the lid of the tomb of Louis de France. 2nd half of 13th century.
(b) *Paris. Musée des Monuments Français*
Tête de Feuilles on the tomb of Louis de France. It is interesting that each of these small heads, one on each corner of the base of the lid, is treated individually.
(c) *Paris. Musée de Cluny*
A harness ornament in gold and enamel. 13th century.

32.   (a) *Noyon (Oise). Cathedral*
Roof boss in the Chapter House. 13th century.
(b) *Noyon (Oise). Cathedral*
Roof boss in the Chapter House. 13th century.

33.   (a) *Mainz. Cathedral*
Tympanum over the Market Portal. 1200–15.
Leaf masks with acanthus sprouting from the mouth and from the upper lip, or nostrils in the ornamental frame.
(b) One of the six leaf masks in the border.

34.   (a) *Worms. Cathedral*
Tympanum (inside the north portal). 1200. (*Bildarchiv Foto-Marburg. No. 20706.*)
(b) *Maria Laach. Abbey*
Capital on portico (forecourt). *circa.* 1230.
Two leaf masks, almost in profile, confront each other and appear as one, in full face view.

35.   *Aschaffenburg. St. Peter and St. Alexander*
Corbel carved by Baumeister Fingerhaut in 1220.

36.   *Gelnhausen. Marienkirche*
Head formed mainly of leaves. *circa* 1235.

37.   *Bamberg. Cathedral*
The Rider Statue. Leaf mask on console (on the right). Carved by the Master mason of Bamberg, *circa* 1237. (*Foto-Limmer. Bamberg.*)

38.   *Bamberg. Cathedral*
Leaf mask. (*Foto-Limmer. Bamberg.*)

39. *Ebrach. Former Cistercian Abbey, now a prison church*
Carvings on the portal. 13th century.
(a) Leaf mask on the keystone of the arch.
(b) Leaf mask on a boss.

40. *Friedburg. Liebfrauenkirche*
Tympanum over door leading to sacristy. *circa* 1290.
(*Bildarchiv Foto-Marburg. No. 9105.*)

41. *Mainz. Altertumsmuseum*
(a) Roof boss. Late 13th or early 14th century. (*Bildarchiv Foto-Marburg. No. 13367.*)
(b) *Würzburg. Deutschhauskirche*
Roof boss. *circa* 1290.

42. *Much Marcle. Herefordshire. St Bartholomew*
Capitals in the nave, carved *circa* 1230–40.
(a) Leaf mask with a squint: "stiff-leaf" ornament.
(b) Leaf mask with barely focused eyes. "Stiff-leaf" ornament.

43. (a) *Wadenhoe, Northamptonshire. St. Mary*
Corbel. 13th century.
Foliate head with one eye slanting. The mouth is shaped rather like a figure of eight.
(b) *Grantham, Lincolnshire. St. Wulfram*
Corbel on the north side of the church, and very weather-worn. 13th century.
A death's head with eyes that seem alive and rolling. The lipless, almost toothless mouth is shaped like a figure of eight, the two loops of the figure closed by the remaining front teeth. Leaves grow through the gaps on either side.

44. (a) *Ripon, Yorkshire. Cathedral*
Corbel in the nave, 13th century.
Grim faced foliate head with a figure of eight mouth.
(b) *Dorchester, Oxfordshire. Abbey*
Foliate head supporting vaulting shaft over doorway in the south-east angle of the Lady Chapel. 13th century.
Vines grow out of the huge, figure of eight mouth – pulled out and twisted into this grotesque shape by pain: it is an expression of human anguish.

45. *Southwell, Nottinghamshire. Minster*
Tympana in the Chapter House. Late 13th century.
(The Tympana are numbered and the plants identified after Seward: see *List of References*, 55.)
(a) Tympanum 3: Buttercup (*Ranunculus*) or Cranesbill (*Geranium pusillum* or possibly *G. sanguineum*). Two leaves growing out of the man's mouth and one on his head.
(b) Tympanum 5: Buttercup and Hops coming from the man's mouth.
(c) Tympanum 12: Buttercup. Two sprays coming from the man's mouth and one growing from his head. Two birds, one pecking a flower.
(d) Tympanum 13: A spray of Ivy coming out of the man's mouth. Two birds: one pecks the stem and the other carries a fledgling in its beak.

46. *Southwell, Nottinghamshire. Minster.*
Tympana in the Chapter House.
(a) Tympanum 14: Two sprays coming from the man's mouth, the one on the left resembles wild apple (*Pyrus malus*) or cherry (*Prunus cerasus*) or blackthorn (*Prunus spinosa*). The spray on the right is probably black bryony (*Tanus communis*) or bitter sweet (*So-lanum dulcamara*) or convolvulus.
(b) Tympanum 22: Maple, with fruit, coming out of the man's mouth.
(c) Tympanum 26: Dragons with linked hawthorn tails. Although this decorative fantasy has no direct connection with the foliate heads represented at Southwell, it reminds us of twelfth century imagery where animal and vegetable forms grow out of each other and are freely interchangeable elements, and either or both, separately or mixed, may come out of the mouths or ears of demon heads. The little dragons, like the Green Men, are used to vary the foliage ornament of the thirty-six tympana.
(d) Tympanum 33: A young man's face peers narrow-eyed and frowning, through a bent-over spray of berried hawthorn which he pulls apart with his hands. The head is not, in this case, the source of the foliage but forms a centre for the design.

47. (a) *Southwell, Nottinghamshire. Minster*
Decoration above the abacus of capital (No. 31).
A hawthorn mask, corresponding to the *Tête de Feuilles*. The capital below is decorated with flowering hawthorn.
(b) *Cadney, Lincolnshire. All Saints*
Corbel. 13th century.
Head with sprays of oak coming from the mouth.
(c) *Southwell, Nottinghamshire. Minster*
Corbel in the Chapter House.
Ivy coming from the mouth on the right, maple on the left.

48. (a) *Noyon Cathedral. (Chapter House)*
Head with vines, and birds stealing the grapes. 13th century.
(b) *Sutton Benger, Wiltshire. All Saints*
The superb Green Man on the western respond is believed to date from the late 13th or early 14th century (Sir Nikolaus Pevsner, *Wiltshire* (1963), in the *Buildings of England* (series) Penguin Books, and personal communication), though it may have been worked on during the restorations of 1851. Two Green Men on the outside of the church are probably of this later date, and are carved "after the style" of the foliate head inside. The plant is hawthorn, and birds peck at the berries. Did the idea come from Noyon?

49. *Exeter, Devon. Cathedral*
Corbel on the north side of the choir: late 13th or early 14th century.

50. *Exeter, Devon. Cathedral*
(a) Roof boss in the Lady Chapel: early 14th century. Silverweed (*Potentilla anserina*) or Mugwort (*Artemisia vulgaris*) grows out of a figure of eight mouth with very irregular teeth.
(b) Roof boss in Retrochoir, early 14th century.
Two heads with Mugwort or Wormwood (*Artemisia absinthium*).

51. (a) *Halse, Somerset. St. James*
Roundel, *circa* 1300, mounted on the north wall, inside the church. Oak leaves come from the nostrils, and another spray grows upwards from the bridge of the nose.
(b) *Claypole, Lincolnshire. St. Peter*
Capital, *circa* 1325.

52. *Harpswell, Lincolnshire, St. Chad*
(a) Effigy of William Harrington, rector. †1350.
(b) Foliate head at the base of the memorial. Large flat leaves grow from the nose and spread over the cheeks, and smaller leaves grow on the forehead.

53. *Winchester, Hampshire. Cathedral*
Spandrel in Choir Stalls. 1308–10.

54. *Winchester, Hampshire. Cathedral*
Spandrel in Choir Stalls. 1308–10.

55. (a) *Beverley, Yorkshire. Minster*
Capital in the nave. 1308–49.
(b) *Lichfield, Staffordshire. Cathedral*
Capital. 1340.
This Green Man, an English "*Tête de Feuilles*", is reputed to be a "portrait" of the King's Master Builder, William de Ramessey.

56. *Leckhampstead, Buckinghamshire. St. Mary the Virgin*
Panel on the font. 14th century.
A spray of oak leaves comes from the mouth of a man's head which is smaller that the leaves and only a little larger than the clusters of acorns.

57. *Ely, Cambridgeshire. Cathedral*
Roof bosses in the Lady Chapel. 1335–53.
C. J. P. Cave (see *List of References*, 3) tells us that when he photographed these roof bosses and discovered faces under the foliage they reminded him of the Jack in the Green he had seen as a boy, peeping through his covering of leaves. The use of the telescopic lens (necessary to photograph these bosses which are some 70 feet high) tends to distort and "flatten" the perspective: the faces are actually more deeply withdrawn behind the foliage that they appear in the photo-graphs, but the photographs allow us to see the expression of the faces more clearly and reveal that most of these Green Men are far from amiable characters.
(a) The eyes are the only clearly visible feature of this face; the rest are hidden in the shadows of the leaves which all rise out of the mouth.
(b) One leaf comes from the mouth but most of the foliage develops from the bulbous nose.

58. *Ely Cathedral.   Chapel*
(a) The arrange   f leaves is the same .
57 (b), but mor   face is exposed.
(b) Leaves grow   ears and from the

59. *Ely Cathedral. Lad,*
(a) A *Tête de Feuilles*   'most feminine features.
(b) Leaves veil, but do i   nceal, the diabolical face of this Green Man whose vicious teeth bite on the thick branches coming out of the mouth.

60. *Ely Cathedral. Lady Chapel*
(a) The most conspicuous feature of this demon (with his face painted green) is his huge tongue (painted red). Leaves grow out of his mouth and ears.
(b) The leaves are disposed peripherally: one pokes out through a gap in the teeth.

61. *Marburg an der Lahn. Elisabethkirche*
Rood Screen. ? *circa* 1349.
There are at least a dozen Green Men on this leafy rood screen; clustered like flowers at the bases of the columns supporting the arch, and round the capital on the left. (*Bildarchiv Foto-Marburg. No. 77384.*)

62. Marburg. Rood Screen
(a) The complete screen. (*Bildarchiv Foto-Marburg. No. 77383.*)
(b) One of the Green M   n. (*Bildarchiv Foto-Marburg. No. 77385.*)

63. *Weston Longville (Norf   ll Saints*
Ornament of the sedilia.   entury.
(a) Face with tongue stickin   . Bra hes grow out of his head, just above the e   ke horns.
(b) Face with branches comin   of the mouth.
(c) Little Man carrying sprays   t and vine.

64. *Bristol. St. Mary Redcliffe*
(a) Corbel. 14th century. The frown li   of this agreeable face develop as the veins of the le   which grow from his brows.
(b) Gilded roof boss. 14th century. A   g Green Man.

65. (a) *Bristol. St Mary Redcliffe*
14th century tained glass in a window (under the Tower) reconstructed in the 19th century.
Only one eye appears: the other is obliterated by the leadin   The large ears suggest that this Green Man is an i   or a demon, an   own might well allude to the   n of Satan (.   84 (a) and (b)).
(b) *Sc   l, Nottingh   Minster*
Miseric   h century

66. *Nantwi   re. St.   y*
(a) Stai   4th century. One of the original lights ren   a window, mostly restored in the 19th centu   ne present vestry (formerly the Lady Chapel). Th   medieval glass at Nantwich was probably made by the Cistercians at Abbey Vale Royal in Delamere Forest.
The mouth and small tongue of this frowning Green Man are feline, but the nose, eyes and ears are human. The pupils of the eyes converge in a squint.
(b) Sandsto   ead carved above the pillar of the arch of the tow   ing north. 14th century.

67. (a) *Covent   y,   arwickshire. Holy Trinity*
Misericord. I   14th or early 15th century.
(b) *Loversall, rkshire. St. Katherine*
Misericord. Late 14th or early 15th century.

68. *Lincoln Cathedral*
(a) Misericord. Late 14th century.
(b) Arm rest in choir stalls. Late 14th century.

69. *Bamberg. Cathedral*
Foliate head in the choir stalls. Late 14th century. (*Bildarchiv Foto-Marburg. No. 6464.*)

70. (a) *Chester Cathedral*
Misericord. 1390.
Demonic Green Man.
(b) *Marburg an der Lahn. Universitätsmuseum*
Roof boss. 2nd half of the 14th century. (*Bildarchiv Foto-Marburg. No. 140144.*)

71. *South Tawton, Devon. St. Andrew*
Roof bosses. 14th or 15th century.
(a) A *Tête de Feuilles* whose expression suggests a state of drunken stupor. A Green Man with a hang-over?
(b) The branches twist like worms round the head of this moribund Green Man. The face wastes away but the grapes are swelling.

72. *South Tawton, Devon. St Andrew*